The Communication Handbook

ACKNOWLEDGEMENTS

It is my pleasure to acknowledge The Association of Image Consultants, International (AICI) for the plethora of information offered at their conferences over the years. My 25+ years of service encouraged me to write this book to embrace the educational opportunities I've been afforded through this association. The association consists of the A, B, C's of Image; this book is about the C – Communications. It is through AICI that I became the first Master Status Recipient in their history, known as AICI CIM.

My special thanks go to cover designer, Victoria Pent, for the illustrations, including the front and back cover and spine and to Anna Marie Rutledge, Image Consultant, who read the book and whose insight helped the final version.

Finally, I need to thank my incredibly supportive husband, Alan, who has been my best friend and mentor for over 46 years. I could never have accomplished all that I have without his belief in me and in my ability to write self-help books.

Also by Dr Joyce Knudsen, Ph.D

Successful Failures: Wisdom for Aspiring Musicians
The Generational Puzzle
From Head to Soul for Women
From Head to Soul for Men
Refusing to Quit: True Stories of Women Over 60
Symbols: The Art of Communication

The Communication Handbook

By

Joyce Knudsen, Ph.D.

TABLE OF CONTENTS

PART ONE

PART TWO

INTRODUCTION

Most people are not getting their message across. While they are sending messages, much is being lost within the communication process, which, according to research, comprises more than 90% of the messages being sent.

Some of the reasons why this may be are as follows:

- The receiver may be thinking about what the right answer would be for your question.
- The receiver may be thinking about something that just happened that they cannot get out of their heads.
- The receiver may have feelings and emotions that they feel are being compromised from listening to the communication.

By the time your message is received and processed by the listener, your message may have lost much of its original intent. The person who "hears" the message will decode it. They are applying their own interpretation to your message.

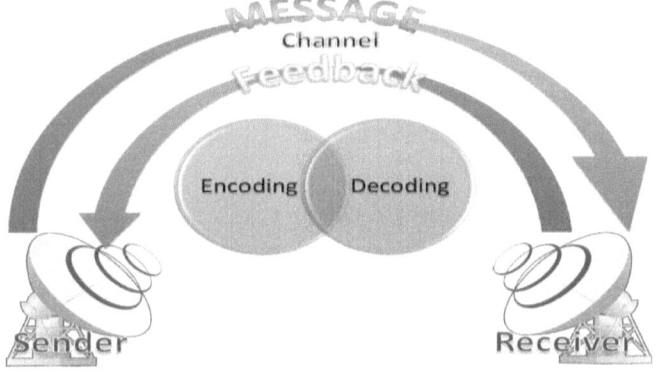

In business and in personal relationships, we want our messages to be both effective and understood, if we are to proceed with good communication between two parties. In this book, it is my hope that you will learn the necessary language skills to communicate effectively.

Everywhere we go, there seems to be messages of some kind. There are signs, logos, labels, photographs, newspapers, mobile devices and computer screens. The messages are so common that we get used to them and instinctively know what they mean.

People interpret what they want to interpret.

In the book, **Words That Work,** Frank L. Luntz wrote: *"It's not what you say, it's what people hear."* He goes on to say *"You can have the best message in the world, but the person on the receiving end will always understand it through the prism of his or her own emotions, preconceptions, prejudices and pre-existing beliefs."*

In today's world of social networking, texting, tweets and Facebook posts, along with many other electronic forms of communication, words can easily be misunderstood and misinterpreted. When sending messages, people want immediate gratification. It used to be that when people wrote letters, they had to wait days for a response. Today, we are able to reach worldwide contacts in seconds. We are living in an era where we connect in "real time."

In the book, **Multiple Intelligences,** Howard Gardner, wrote: *"We now have the opportunity to go beyond stated expectations and explore specific interests. Since sending and receiving messages immediately is so beneficial, we* *seem to have lost the ability to use more archaic forms of communication. No longer do your children call every week; they text. Everything has moved in a direction of 'I need information right now.' It concerns me we are losing the opportunity to communicate in-person or over a landline, in lieu of technological advances."*

Edward R. Murrow said, *"Communication is the process of exchanging information and ideas. An active process, it involves encoding, transmitting, and decoding intended messages. There are many means of communicating and many different language systems. Speech and language are only a portion of communication. Other aspects of communication may enhance or even eclipse the linguistic code. These aspects are paralinguistic, nonlinguistic and linguistic. It is the transmission of information so that the recipient understands what the sender intends."*

Somewhere in-between the sender and the receiver are the thought processes and feelings that allow the receiver to make their own interpretations. The receiver must be open to receiving the sender's message, if communication is to be effective.

For example, when we see a yellow sign with a curved arrow along the road, we know there is a curve ahead. When we see a plus sign, we know we are to add something. When we see a red light, we know to stop.

The key to understanding communication is that both the sender and receiver have a mutual understanding of what is being said. Let's say that you were given a math problem, but you did not know the minus sign is the signal for subtraction. You would be unable to complete the math problem.

When people actually wrote letters with a pen and paper they were forced to wait until the receiver was able to respond. Therefore, communication was delayed due to time constraints. Now, there is more immediacy in our communication. Because communication is at the core of what we do, this book has been written in order to explore the communication process and all its various complications.

I've divided this book into two parts.
Part One explains the forms of communication and why they are important.

Part Two includes narratives of well-known people, who had to communicate to mass audiences.

In learning how to effectively communicate, verbally and non- verbally, we will create more effective communication in all of our relationships.

I've enjoyed writing this book in an attempt to make sense of the communication process and all of its nuances. It is my hope you will enjoy reading this book as much as I enjoyed writing it. Enjoy the book!

~Dr. Joyce Knudsen, Ph.D.

PART ONE

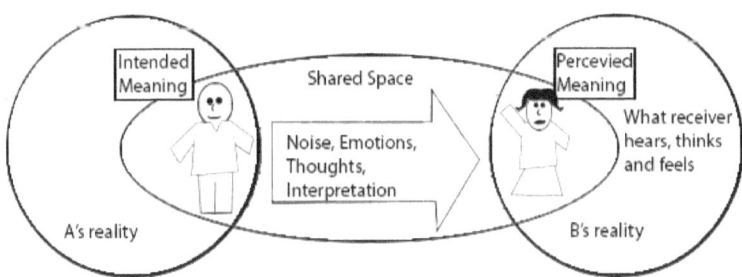

We send a message with an intended meaning, which is one person's reality. Then, somewhere in-between, there is some shared space, with noise, emotions, thoughts and interpretations. Another person's reality is what they perceive the message to be. It is what the person receiving the message hears, thinks and feels.

Are we communicating and getting our message across? Not always!

HUMAN THOUGHT AND COMMUNICATION

"Developing excellent communication skills is absolutely essential to effective leadership. The leader must be able to share knowledge and ideas to transmit a sense of urgency and enthusiasm to others. If a leader can't get a message across clearly and motivate others to act on it, then having a message doesn't even matter."— Gilbert Amelio, President and CEO of National Semiconductor Corp

Somewhere along the line, an idea was formed to indicate that human beings communicated from learning from philosophers.

These philosophers had discovered that words, if chosen correctly,
were fundamental to effective communication.

Companies with more than 50,000 employees researched found that communication was the single decisive factor in choosing managers for corporations. Professor Albert Mehrabian knew the importance of communication He studied body language and nonverbal communication. His findings provided the basis effective communication.

Mehrabian's findings are:

- 7% of meaning is in the spoken word.

- 38% is how the words are said.

- 55% show up on facial expressions.

There was a NY Times article (4/8/86) by Daniel Goleman, entitled, *Studies Point to Power of Nonverbal Signals,* reporting on research by Peter Blanck, which said:

"How a judge gives his instructions to a jury was perceived to double the likelihood that the jury would deliver a verdict of guilty, or not guilty -- even when on the surface the judge's demeanor seemed perfectly impartial."

THE COMMUNICATION PROCESS

It is putting your thoughts into words!

Communication is divided into three main categories, 1) verbal, 2) nonverbal, and 3) paralanguage. The verbal content is what we say. The content given in a nonverbal context is one we send with our bodies; our reaction to what is being said and Paralanguage is a component of communication that may modify the meaning of the message, or convey emotion through the use of intonation, pitch and other factors. All three types of communication must be visible, in order to send a concise message.

The person being sent the message (receiver) must understand messages the person sending (sender) is communicating. Most of what is "heard" is our nonverbal message; this form of communication is something we do physically. An example would be if someone was talking to you and the other person rolled their eyes or looked away. These are signals people give, unknowingly, that can help you to understand the communication process and how to work it well. Our use of our language could show great power during the problem-solving process. Words need to be chosen carefully to minimize problems or there is an associative risk that may result in resistance. Sentences beginning with *"As you probably know . . ."* or *"I know you are familiar with ..."* will often evoke a positive response.

If you want to send an effective message, you need to state your point of view as quickly and succinctly as you can. Make your messages clear and concise by your use of the language (all three!)

WHAT IS COMMUNICATION?

It is putting your thoughts into words! When you communicate, you use pauses, a certain tone, speak loudly or softly in order to enhance the spoken word. Communicating via speeches, telephone, discussions, face to face or even voicemail is defined as the spoken language.

People use written communication when they want something more formal to keep as a record of what they said. Written communication is formal, such as a letter to document an interview or conversation. Although this type of communication may be considered impersonal, it serves a purpose. Using this form of communication to get immediate feedback, such as the opportunity to ask questions when the meaning is not entirely clear.

VERBAL COMMUNICATION

Verbal communication is the act of expressing your thoughts with words. It is generally defined as spoken language. Tone, enunciation, pauses, loudness, emphasis, word choice are all in use when speaking to enhance the spoken word.

If there is at least one sender and one person to receive a message, the word that is spoken is considered an example of verbal and impersonal communication.

Communication in this way helps one to receive immediate feedback and gives the receiver an opportunity to ask questions. 'Word of mouth' comes from this form of communication.

Research suggests that most communication models have some sort of feedback that is verbal from the person receiving the message. This could be something as insignificant as an 'Uh-huh.'

Examples of this type of verbal communication are speeches, face-to-face discussions, telephone conversations, voicemail, television, radio, seminars, or videos. People using sign language would be considered to be using a form of verbal communication. In a broader sense verbal communication would also include the written word. That may include letters, faxes, emails, books, newspapers, magazines, articles, hand written notes or announcements.

There could be a considerable difference between written and spoken communication. People use written communication when they want something more formal to keep as a record of what they said.

A form of verbal communication is written. Written communication is formal, such as a letter to document an interview or conversation during a meeting. Although this type of communication may be considered impersonal, it serves a purpose. Using this form of communication helps you to get immediate feedback such as the opportunity to ask questions when the meaning is not entirely clear.

COMMON ERRORS IN VERBAL COMMUNICATION
There are so many errors people make in the communication process and this can be an indicator of poor English Skills. Some examples are:

The words *loose* and *lose* are two different words, but most people do not recognize this.
Your and *You're* are two different words; most people do not recognize this.

There, Their and *They* are three different words; however, they are often used interchangeably.

Affect is a verb and *effect* is a noun.

An *apostrophe* is not necessarily plural.

Literally means *it happened*; not figuratively.

The word *it's* is short for *'It is.'* And *Its* means *"belonging to it."*

Acute means *"sharp,"* as in an acute illness; it rapidly gets worse and reaches a crisis vs. a *chronic* illness, which may be severe, but has a long-lasting or lingering effect.

Adverse means *"unfavorable, contrary* or *hostile"* while *averse* means *"having a strong feeling of opposition, antipathy or repugnance."*

Many people use these words, and other words, incorrectly. If you are going to speak, you must research correct meanings of the words you use – otherwise your message can be lost in the translation.

Using our voice involves so much knowledge and correct pronunciation of words.

THE USE OF PARAPHRASING

When communicating, there is a sender (person relaying the message) and receiver (person sender is talking to.) The problem occurs when the sender is not communicating effectively to the receiver. Feelings, emotions and perceptions get in the way of the sender getting the message. The receiver has his/her mind on something else. To be sure a message is received, one needs to develop the art of being able to paraphrase what has been said.

Through the use of paraphrasing, we can be sure that the message has been sent. We all work with people who have different opinions, values, beliefs and needs, which can affect our ability to exchange ideas and understand another person's perspective.

To be sure your message is transmitted effectively to the receiver, paraphrase. What is paraphrasing? Paraphrasing is merely the act of restating what has been said. For example, "As I understand it, you are in a lost place and need some help with your image, is this correct?" Use fact, not opinion when paraphrasing.

Always be sure to clarify to the person in this way, so both of you are on the 'same page.' You may ask the sender to explain their behavior. Be certain to keep your questions open.

For example: "When I was debriefing your report, you seemed excited. Are you happy about the result? Let me see if I understand what you said."

At times, messages can be difficult to listen to when they seem to blame, label or judge people or things, which may or may not be true. (Many times they are not true.) Always change messages to 'I' messages.

"I feel angry" or "I don't understand," indicate approachability.

"A significant amount of communication occurs through body language. Though we can't see our own, everyone else does. If

you're saying one thing and thinking another, your body language may well give you away."
~Gerri King, Ph.D.
COMMUNICATION TIPS

May I? - When you ask permission, you imply the person has authority.

As you of course know... - You will be affirming that this person has great knowledge of the subject.

Could you give me your advice? - This says that you recognize their superior wisdom and value their opinion. You have lifted them to a higher level of expertise.

I would appreciate it if... - You have implied that he or she has the power to grant or refuse and you need their help.

You are so right. - What a pat on the back. Everyone wants to be right. Who won your last argument?

Can you spare time from your busy life? - You are recognizing how important this person is and how valuable each minute can be. You are respecting their time.

Using these phrases helps the listener feel good about what they already know and this is a solid first-step for them to listen further.

NONVERBAL COMMUNICATION

Open, relaxed position Smiling facial expression Widened pupils Good eye contact	**Positive Signals**
Crossed arms & legs Constricted pupils Pulling away Lack of eye contact	**Negative Signals**

We are judged over 90% on what we do not say!

Kinesics, body language and nonverbal communication describe the body movements in addition to sounds and tones. When we speak, often times, this can be involuntary and many times, difficult to distinguish.

Movement, gestures and poses intentionally made by a person (i.e., conscious smiling, hand movements and imitation) are voluntary communication.

Generally, movement made with some sort of intention, along with an understanding of what it communicates can be considered voluntary. Something such as a facial expression would be considered involuntary body language, which can convey emotion.

This form of language is important when groups are involved. Body language includes movements, such as a nod of the head or a rising of the eyebrows and movement of the entire body, such as overall body tension or jumping up and down. It is not always easy to perceive different meanings of body language, because this involves interpretation.

If someone came into your office and was frowning, you might interpret that they are in a bad mood, but the look could be very unintentional. You unconsciously widen your eyes when you see something pleasant, exciting or arousing. Non-reflexive body language can be much more difficult to interpret.

In fact, we learn many subtle variations of each of these gestures and use them when called for in a given situation. We use our head to say 'yes' or 'no,' to smile, frown and wink acknowledgement or flirtation. Our head and shoulder in combination may shrug to indicate that we do not know something.

Albert Mehrabian knew the importance of communication He studied body language and nonverbal communication. His findings provided the basis effective communication.

His findings as stated before, but worth repeating were:

- 7% of meaning is in the spoken word.
- 38% is how the words are said.
- 55% shows up on facial expressions.

Some forms of nonverbal communication would be foot movements, voice variations and facial expressions. We may not be verbally calling someone a bad name, but we may send the message non-verbally, without realizing it.

There is often a discrepancy between the words that are being said and that person's physical actions. This can be quite confusing for the receiver.

Words can be manipulated, but gestures are harder to control. Dr. Albert E. Scheflen noticed this lack of communication occurring when he studied people in small groups.

It has been noted that people with power seem to appear larger and stronger and have a more relaxed posture. They don't feel they have to impress anyone. A show of superiority can be a signal. Some examples are: Leaning back in their chairs, gesturing, sitting while others stand, and talking more in louder voices and a tendency to interrupt others.

Studies have shown that people generally stiffen or "freeze up" when lying. If a person barely moves when they speak, this may indicate lying. Defensive and rejection postures include: Folded arms held to the chest and crossed leg. These serve as "clues" to whether a person may not be forthcoming.

Keep in mind that not all people who use these gestures are telling a half-truth or a lie. To some, this is their natural stance. Thus, it is important not to judge people immediately when seeing these postures. You may have to talk to these people more than once to form an accurate impression.

Size and height in the mind of a person can be associated with power. Whatever the mind perceives is important; this may be judged as large. Therefore, anyone who seems larger than life in the mind is liable to be perceived large in your eyes.

Smaller people may have a feeling of insecurity, which may make them defensive around taller people. Sidney Portney, psychologist, found that among smaller people, many had trouble agreeing on the issues presented to them. However, when taller men were added to their group, they grew noticeably ill at ease and argumentative.

The challenge of being taken seriously...the body language learned growing up is often "apologetic." This will not lend itself to being taken seriously and moving into leadership positions.

GESTURES
Another communication that is nonverbal are the gestures we choose to use in our conversations. Gestures are deliberate movements and signals that are communicating some meaning without words. Common gestures include waving, pointing, and using fingers to indicate number amounts. The less you use gestures, the more powerful you will be perceived.

Gestures such as nail biting, rubbing your hands together or chewing gum put you in a lower socio-economic scale according to many experts. Our body postures can create a feeling of warm openness or cold rejection. When someone is facing us with their hands folded in their lap, a feeling of anticipation and interest is being created during this communication. A posture of arms crossed on the chest may portray a feeling of inflexibility (but, not always.) There are some people who only are comfortable doing this with their arms and are very open.

If you want to look younger, stand up straight. According to the
research, unless illness or injury affect your posture, and you cannot stand up straight, you can make a difference in external appearance and internal functioning of body organs with good posture. Posture could reveal our feelings toward a person and/or a situation. Status is often expressed through posture, particularly the status of relationships between a superior and a subordinate. Generally, people use a relaxed postural style

with higher status, while a more upright and tense postural style is reserved for lower status members.

PARALANGUAGE

Like it or not, much of the messages we send face to face are sent through the use of paralanguage and these are bound in various cultures.

When we communicate in our

18

global world, there is the possibility of a misunderstanding taking place. We must send our verbal, paralanguage and our nonverbal messages consistently. If we do not, we confuse the listener; often times this inconsistency can indicate a lack of trust in some people and will undermine the opportunity to build a solid relationship.

If there is conflicting communication, what is going to be believed as the nonverbal message? If you see someone, for example, who has a clenched fist and they tell you they are not angry, you know they are!

Our ability to send accurate, conscious messages is just as important as our ability to receive the messages others send us.

Through conscious attention to verbal messages, and the nonverbal aspects of our words, we are better able to communicate and get our thoughts and feelings heard. And perhaps more importantly, our needs met.

COMMUNICATION, THOUGHTS & BODY LANGUAGE

The Two Roles In Communication:

Sender: The person giving the information

Receiver: The person listening and interpreting the information

How a person perceives the information being said can also depend on interference involved. If the receiver is hungry or tired (or a similar type of interference) they may interpret the message incorrectly.

Nonverbal communication is comprised of many components. We communicate through how we talk, our hand movements, the sounds make, our head movements, our eye movements or even how close or far we stand near someone, our physical appearance, our facial expressions, our posture and body contact, such as shaking hands.

Also, how the receiver perceives the information can depend on many factors with interference as one of these. If the receiver is hungry or tired (or a similar interference), they may perceive what the sender is saying as something different.

In the diagram, two men are communicating about a presentation. The Sender (left) is trying to politely give some suggestions to the Receiver (right).

The Sender thinks the presentation is great, and just needs a couple of changes. The Receiver does not interpret this correctly and perceives the Sender as criticizing his work. The intention of the sender to the receiver has not been conveyed.

The role of sender and receiver switch back and forth throughout the conversation, depending on who is speaking.

KINESICS

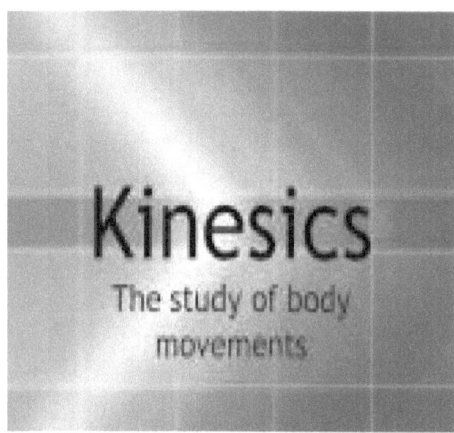

Kinesics or otherwise known as body language describes the body movements in addition to sounds and tones. When we speak, often times, this can be involuntary and many times, difficult to distinguish.

Movement, gestures and poses intentionally made by a person (i.e., conscious smiling, hand movements and imitation) are voluntary communication.

Generally, movement made with some sort of intention, along with an understanding of what it communicates can be considered voluntary.

Something such as a facial expression would be considered involuntary body language, which can convey emotion. This form of language is important when groups are involved.

Body language includes movements, such as a nod of the head or a rising of the eyebrows and movement of the entire body, such as overall body tension or jumping up and down.

It is not always easy to perceive different meanings of body language, because this involves interpretation.

If someone came into our office and was frowning, you might interpret that they are in a bad mood, but the look could be very unintentional. You unconsciously widen your eyes when you see something pleasant, exciting or arousing. Non-reflexive body language can be much more difficult to interpret.

In fact, we learn many subtle variations of each of these gestures and use them when called for in a given situation. We use our head to say 'yes' or 'no,' to smile, frown and wink acknowledgement or flirtation. Our head and shoulder in combination may shrug to indicate that we do not know something.

There is just so much going in within the communication process (as shown in the picture on page 28) that it's difficult to get any message across! As you can see, there are motivating factors, timing issues, role expectations, competition and so much more interfering with the sender's message.

OCULESICS

Oculesics is the word used for eye-contact. This involves the study of eye gaze and pupil dilation.

Studies have found that people use their eyes to indicate their interest and with more than the frequently recognized actions of winking and slight movement of the eyebrows.

Eye contact is an event when two people look at each other's eyes at the same time.

Frequency and interpretation of eye contact vary between cultures and species. Eye aversion is the avoidance of eye contact.

Eye contact and facial expressions provide important social and emotional information. People, perhaps without consciously doing so, probe each other's eyes and faces for positive or negative mood signs.

This is the science behind the movement of the human eye. An example would be people in a group forming a circle. They would rather speak to someone farther away from them than to people close to them.

It is proven that we blink less and dilate more, when our interest heightens. Contraction takes place if we do not!

At the University of Colorado in Boulder, eye contact became a social issue. A student hired an attorney after being banned from campus for staring at several women in the school cafeteria. The

women, who were the recipients of the steady stares, complained that this behavior from a complete stranger was unsettling.

However, the banned student and his attorney claimed that a person has the constitutional right to stare at another person. If you try to stare at another person, or have another person stare at you, you can see how uncomfortable this is.

People do not like stares

It is very difficult to talk to someone when they do not look you in the eye. It makes a person feel as though the person communicating does not care about you or the conversation.

In interpersonal and group communication, we generally are communicating something by looking or not looking at someone.

When eye contact does occur, it may perform one or more functions. The eyes can indicate thought processes, or the cognitive function.

It is common for many people to glance away when they are thinking. Eyes can also perform a monitoring function.

From interpersonal to public speaking situations, we can monitor our communication effectiveness by looking at others and monitoring their feedback. Eye contact also helps to regulate the flow of communication.

If a professor asks a question and you did not wish to respond, you will most likely avoid establishing eye contact; direct eye contact suggests a willingness to respond.

The eyes can also offer insight to emotions and feelings as part of their expressive function. Eyes, it appears, are always "talking" and providing valuable clues.

Normal eye contact means communication is open.

Eyes that are looking down often "say" rejection. Avoiding eye contact suggests someone does not feel secure or included.

A stare can mean dislike

Research continues to show that eye movement can indicate a lot about the person talking.

PUADS SIZE

PUPIL SIZE
Many people have stood by a mirror and have seen the effects of varying amounts of light on their pupil size. Nevertheless, have you ever noticed differences in your pupil size in various situations?

We can control the size of the pupils with light, but are unable to consciously control pupil dilation and constriction. For this reason, our true feelings and emotions usually reveal themselves in the depth of another person's eyes.

Two of the first people to study this concept were Eckhard Hess and James Polt (University of Chicago). They found that pupils enlarged when people were presented a positive stimulus (muscle men and babies for women and nude females for men).

Further research also supported Hess's findings that dilation occurs when positive stimulus or things are interesting to them.

A technique for recording such changes has been developed and preliminary results with cats and human beings are reported, with attention being given to differences between the sexes in response to particular types of material. It's important to note that people are more attracted to others with enlarged pupils.

HAPTICS

Haptics is the study of touch. Communicating through touch is another important nonverbal behavior.

There has been a substantial amount of research on the importance of touch in infancy and early childhood.

Harry Harlow's classic monkey study demonstrated how the deprivation of touch and contact impedes development.

Also, studies done in many hospitals indicate that people who are touched during treatment recover more quickly.

Touch that can be defined as communication includes handshakes, holding hands, kissing (cheek, lips, and hand), back slap, 'high-five,' shoulder pat, brushing arm, etc.

Each symbol sends a nonverbal message as to the touching person's intentions or feelings.

They also cause feelings in the receiver, whether they are positive or negative.

A good handshake is universal and web to web as illustrated here:

OLFACTICS

Did you think there would be a communication defining smell? People have a certain smell and of course, we react to smells, such as body odor. This has a very negative effect on people.

In American culture, the tendency is to cover body odors replacing them with perfume.

In cultures other than America, natural smells are often preferred and considered important in interpersonal communication.

There have been studies about smell due to the fact that smell can have a major effect on our mood, stress reduction, self-confidence sleep enhancement and cognitive and physical performance. There are many factors in the study of smell whether it is adapting to smell, remembering a smell or even discriminating against a certain smell, such as cat odor!

According to *The Smell Report*, smell is not just a biological and psychological experience; it is also a social and cultural phenomenon.

The study of olfaction, previously of interest only in specialist medical research and experimental psychology, is now attracting ever-increasing numbers of anthropologists, sociologists and historians.

In popular culture, the current aromatherapy-boom indicates a similar revival of interest in the powers of perfume.

Once regarded as obscure hippie/new-age mumbo-jumbo, aromatherapy is now respectably 'mainstream.' (Scientists insist that there is still no proof of the benefits of aromatherapy, but the fragrances are undeniably pleasant, which may be enough for most ordinary mortals.)

The findings of research on olfaction, previously reported only in obscure academic journals, now appear regularly in popular newspapers and glossy magazines.

Even the world of technology, so long obsessed with audio-visual-tactile processes, has recently turned its attention to the mysteries of this phenomenon.

CHRONEMICS

Chronemics is the study of our use of time, such as pausing and waiting. The manipulation of time communicates a message.

We all know of the ten minute late arrivals and larger than life egos.

Conversely, individuals who arrive religiously on-time convey an altogether differing message.

But, too, the time people arrive at appointments varies culturally. Customs, social situations and relative status are indicative representations of time and culture in communications.

In North America, if you have a business meeting scheduled, the time you should arrive largely depends on the power relationship between you and the person who you are meeting. People who are lower in stature are expected to arrive on time, if not early. Higher stature individuals can expect others will wait for them if they are late.

For instance, most people who have medical appointments are expected to arrive early and to wait patiently for their doctor to see them rather than the other way around. However, an invitation to a party is an entirely different matter – arriving early is perceived as desperate, so it is often expected most guests will arrive 'fashionably late.'

It generally takes a child at least 12 years to master the subtle cultural aspects of time. By 5 to 6 years of age, children usually know the days of the week, difference between day and night and morning and afternoon as well as meals and nap time. By 7 to 8 years of age, most children can consistently use the clock to tell time.

However, it is not until 12 years of age or older that children begin to comprehend situational aspects of time, such as when to arrive at a party.

When people come together with very different cultural expectations about time, there is a potential for misunderstanding, frustration and hurt feelings. This can occur, for instance, if a Brazilian business man or woman does not arrive 'on time' for a meeting with a New Yorker and fails to provide an apology when he or she does arrive. For the Brazilian, time may be relatively 'elastic' because their pace-of-life is a bit slower.

A Brazilian believes he or she was sufficiently prompt for a scheduled business meeting, having arrived within a half hour of an appointment time.

It is not surprising then, he or she would be astonished and perhaps even offended when he or she is treated coldly by New Yorkers who may feel slighted by a perception of rudeness or disconcerting behavior.

Distances at which each individual feels comfortable interacting can compound these misunderstandings. A scenario such as this can be avoided, of course, by foreknowledge about other cultures and willingness to adopt cultural relativity in business applications.

The old saying, "When in Rome do as the Romans do," remains excellent advice.

PROXEMICS

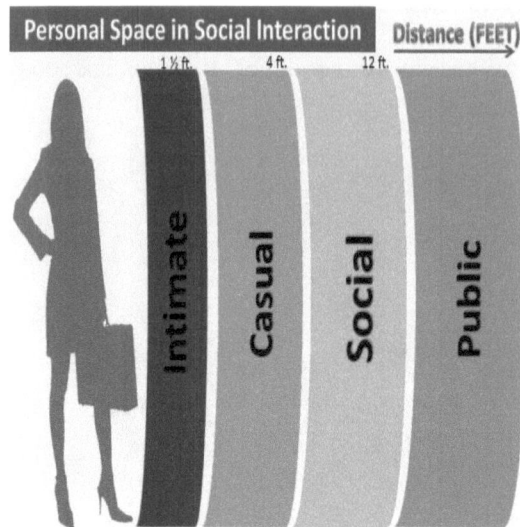

Edward Hall, a researcher studied space, and how various differences in that use can make us feel more relaxed or more anxious.

Proxemics can be described in terms of physical territory, such as a classroom placement of objects in this territory communicates and effects behavior. For example, desks that face the front of a classroom rather than towards a center-aisle, affect our ability to send and receive messages. Even the arrangement of desks communicates certain messages on its own.

There is a certain amount of space (proximity) that you keep between yourself and another person. In terms of physical territory, there are some very important matters to consider:

Spatial relationships even the shape of a table, encourage different types of interaction. When teaching students, it is generally a good idea to sit them in a circular style so that each person has an equal chance to see everything, hear everything and participate.

Various cultures suggest to us how to organize space in such a way as to control the nature of interaction. In North American corporate offices, for instance, the boss is usually physically isolated in a very separate private room. This tends to minimize his or her personal contact with ordinary workers. In contrast, Japanese offices commonly are set up with the boss's desk at the end of a row of pushed together desks used by subordinate employees. This maximizes his interaction with them.

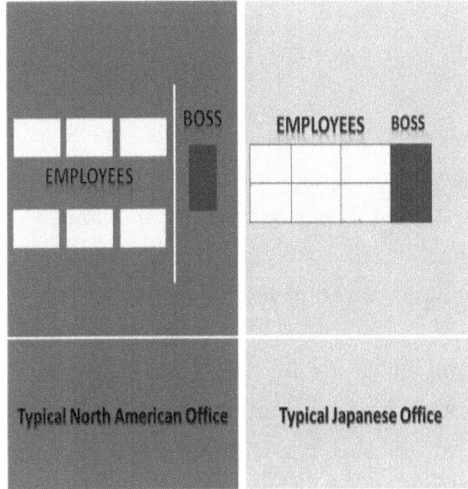

Typical North American Office   Typical Japanese Office

The exhibit (left) shows an example of a cultural adaptation in the communication in an office setting.

A courtroom similarly alters behavior; in the United States, the judge usually wears a black robe and sits behind an elevated desk. The other desks and chairs in court are positioned so attention is focused on the judge.

This intentional setting makes those present feel respectful and subservient to the judge, thereby making it easier for him or her to control the proceedings.

Culture also guides perceptions of space by defining its units. In the industrial world, space is divided into standardized segments with sides and positions. Acres and city lots with uniform dimensions are examples of this.

Property boundaries are referenced to segments of space. As the density of population increases, the importance of defined spatial boundaries grows. Land owners in densely occupied neighborhoods have been known to get angry enough to kill one another over disputed segmented boundaries or 'fence lines' between properties. In less dense, more rural areas of the American landscape, where people tend to own ranches of hundreds and even thousands of acres, the movement of a fence three feet one way or another is rarely consequential – unless there are significant mining rights or access points adversely affected by such a move.

Personal Space

The amount of distance we need, and the amount of space we perceive as belonging to us is influenced by a number of factors. These include level of familiarity, personality characteristics, situational factors and social norms.

The amount of personal space needed when having a casual conversation with another person usually varies between 18 inches to four feet. On the other hand, the personal distance needed when speaking to a crowd of people is around 10 to 12 feet.

A generalized example pulled from many resources follow:

Personal Zone -
0'- 1 ½' – actually touching or of distance to be easily touched

Social Zone -
1 ½' – 4' – arm length with the ability to shake hands

Public Zone -
4'- 10' – works with business

The more we get to know one another, the more we are permitted into each another person's personal space.

Executives, presidents of colleges, government officials have large offices with big spaces and their assistants typically have smaller spaces – thus, space communicates their position as well as level of comfort.

DISTANCE BETWEEN FACES	TONE OF VOICE	TYPE OF MESSAGE
very close (3-6")	soft whisper	top secret or sensual
close (8-12")	audible whisper	very confidential
neutral (20-36")	soft voice, low volume	personal subject matter
neutral (4.5-5')	full voice	non-personal information
across the room (8-20')	loud voice	talking to a group
stretching the limits (20-24' indoors and up to 100' outdoors)	loud hailing voice	departures and arrivals
Derived from The Silent Language by Edward Hall (1959)		

Our personal space is the amount of air, which surrounds us, and is considered by our unconscious as our own.

In an experiment, couples were asked to walk toward one another while conversing and stop when they reached a comfortable conversational distance. Then he gave each couple a test to measure marital intimacy, desire for change and potential for divorce. He discovered a relationship between distance and happiness. Happy couples stood 11.4 inches apart while distressed couples stood 14.8 inches apart. The distance between distressed couples was 25% greater than the happy couples.

We react negatively to someone who invades our space.

For example, if someone comes too close for your personal space, you may step back to a distance you are more comfortable with.

People forced to invade one another's space, such as on an elevator or subway, show an uncomfortable mindset. You may notice them turning their heads or watching numbers on the display for their floor – they want to get off as quickly as possible.

When you are in someone's office, it is not okay to put your briefcase on someone's desk. That is their personal space. When we speak to another individual or group, the distance our bodies are physically apart also communicates a message. Most of us are unaware of the importance of space in communication until we are confronted with someone who uses it differently.

For instance, we all have a sense of what is a comfortable interaction distance to a person with whom we are speaking. If that person gets closer than the distance at which we are comfortable, we usually back up to re-establish our comfort zone. Similarly, if we feel that we are too far away from the person we are talking to, we are likely to close the distance between us. If two speakers have different levels of comfortable interaction distances, a ballet of shifting positions usually occurs until one of the individual is backed into a corner and feels threatened by what may be perceived as hostile or sexual overtures. As a result, the verbal message may not be listened to or understood as it was intended.

In Latin America, the comfortable (ideal) interaction distance for discussing personal topics is often significantly closer than among Non-Latinos. Comfort in interaction distance mostly has to do with distance between faces looking directly at one another. The nature of the message communicated also affects interaction distances.

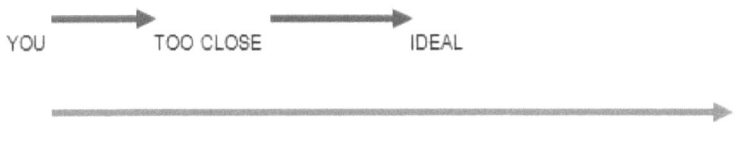

Average comfortable distances among North Americans

GENDER DIFFERENCES

When traveling to other societies, it is also important to understand there are likely to be significant gender differences in communication in addition to distinctions in clothes and adornment. Again, in America, men prefer face-to-face conversation and maintain direct eye contact longer than other cultures.

In contrast, women often converse standing side-by-side but closer together than men typically do. Male handshakes tend to be firmer.

American women usually are restrained in the use of bold gestures but use more facial expressions (especially smiles) and are more skilled in interpreting them.

In Japan, women most often speak with an artificially high pitch, especially when conversing with men in a business or official setting. This is part of the general deference traditionally shown to men. However, recent research indicates the pitch of female voices in Japan has begun to lower.

It has been suggested this change is connected with increased economic and political clout of Japanese women. Except in moments of intimacy or formal greeting (hand shaking or hugging), this informal rule is most rigidly applied to men.

Similar culturally defined patterns of physical contact avoidance are found in most of the cultures of Asia and Northern Europe. In Southern Europe, the Middle East and Latin America, much more physical contact is expected and desired. Your space expands and contracts, depending on the situation. The amount of space a person controls is associated with that person's degree of status.

The next time you are at a professional's office, such as a doctor, lawyer or accountant, look at the size of their desk. This may not be an accident!

FACIAL EXPRESSION

There are many types of facial expressions that are evident in all cultures. They are anger, fear, disgust, joy, surprise and sadness.

These expressions are an important channel of nonverbal communication. Many animal species display facial expressions, but expressions are highly developed particularly in the primates, and perhaps most of all, in humans.

Even though the human species has acquired the powerful capabilities of a verbal language, the role of facial expressions in person-to-person interactions remain substantial. Messages of the face that provide commentary and illustration about verbal communications are significant in themselves.

These types of expressions provide a different mode for understanding the private, hidden side of the inner person, a side that may not be accessible in the form of verbalizations. Such emotion indicators range from stereotyped, full-face expressions that are obvious to fleeting, partial-face movements that are hard to see.

Facial expressions and the ability to understand them are important for successful interpersonal relations, so improving these skills is often sought out.

Consider how much information can be conveyed with a smile or a frown. There are so many muscles in one's face and they are known to create approximately seven thousand expressions.

Facial expressions are also crucial in the nonverbal process. There are many types of facial expressions that are evident in all cultures. They are anger, fear, disgust, joy, surprise and sadness.

These expressions are an important channel of nonverbal communication. Many animal species display facial expressions, but expressions are highly developed particularly in the primates, and perhaps most of all, in humans.

Even though the human species has acquired the powerful capabilities of a verbal language, the role of facial expressions in person-to-person interactions remains substantial.

Messages of the face that provide commentary and illustration about verbal communications are significant in themselves.

These types of expressions provide a different mode for understanding the private, hidden side of the inner person, a side this may not be accessible in the form of verbalizations.

Such emotion indicators range from stereotyped, full-face expressions that are obvious to fleeting, partial-face movements that are hard to see.

COLOR

With a demonstrable effect on communication, colors result in automatic reactions. In fact, 60% of the way we judge and are judged has to do with color. Also, men and women respond differently to color.

Did you know?
-   Sugar will not sell in a green package?
-   Beauty aids in brown jars do not sell?
-   Children want cereal in red or yellow boxes?
-   Charcoal gray and navy blue send an 'unspoken' message,
    which says… reliable… credible… "You can count on me."

Colors can have a major impact on our comfort level in a given situation.

A study by the Ketchum public relations firm showed using three different colors in the same room create very different results.

Their study included one school, which was not painted; one school, which was left in the usual scheme of buff walls and white ceilings;

Dependable
mysterious
Lucky
Vibrant
Dignified
POWERFUL
Happy

BLUE
BLACK
GREEN
ORANGE
PURPLE
RED
YELLOW

and one school with color dynamics used   pale rose classrooms and green chalk boards.

Their study and results were resolute - color works. In the school
with dynamic color there was improvement in multiple variables, such as health, safety, scholastic aptitude and social habits among arts, language, math, music and science.

Perhaps even more important than our unconscious reactions to color are those connections we make between color and conscious ideas.

There are meanings we ascribe to colors as symbols. For instance, kings wear royal purple robes to designate power and men wear uniforms to denote an army they belong to. In ancient tribes, the colors a man wore were indicative of leadership roles and prominence.

SYMBOLIC MEANINGS OF COLOR:

Symbolic Meanings of Color		
Color	Moods	Messages
Red	Hot, Excitement	Happiness, Blood
Blue	Cool, Leisure	Dignity, Truth
Yellow	Joyful, Cheerful	Glamour, Brightness
Orange	Stimulating, Defiant	Harvest, Thoughtfulness
Purple	Stately, Dignified	Wisdom, Victory
Green	Cool, In Control	Security, Peace
Black	Intense, Anxiety	Mystery, Power
Brown	Melancholy, Neutral	Protection, Atonement
White	Joy, Light, Cold	Purity, Innocence

Color carries communicates messages beyond the mere fact of color itself. Colors can be used strategically to communicate well.

VOLACAICS

Volacaics is a reference to the tone of our voice, be it high, low, quick or slow.

If you say to someone, *"Are you here,"* in a rising tone that is descending. This acts as a nonverbal cue.

Listeners decide your age, intelligence, qualifications, sense of humor and more from the way you speak.

How often have you heard someone say, "I only spoke to Tom for a minute, but he sounds like a nice guy" or "Phyllis called and she certainly did sound upset."

Of course, we judge these qualities in part by what was said; however, we also judge by the way they were said. What are we listening to? Naturally, ideas and information are important.

Beyond that, the voice has many aspects to consider such as Articulation - how clearly you sound out your words. Enunciate to avoid sounding uneducated, lazy or indifferent. Do not overdo this.

Cultural interpretations and uses of time, body motion, proxemics and touch help to develop and determine behavior. Biorhythm theory suggests that people are affected by physical, sensitivity and intellectual cycles.

Either person can offer the first handshake in business. The person who offers this is at an advantage because they are showing control and taking the initiative and being direct. This makes a good impression.

Use direct eye contact. If your handshake is refused, then withdraw your hand discreetly.

If this happens, you have gained valuable information about the person who refused the handshake. The person is resentful, angry or distracted.

Do not give a limp handshake because it will indicate lack of character, enthusiasm, confidence and hostility. If you get a limp handshake from a person who normally gives you a firm one, this may indicate some change in the relationship.

Never crush someone with a handshake that is too forceful. This will indicate insecurity suggesting he or she is showing whose boss.

Two-handed handshakes are condescending, especially if the recipient's hand is turned over horizontally.

SPEAKING & PROJECTION

Learning effective speaking skills will not only help you in your career, but will help in everyday life activities.

The following are guidelines to speaking:

PITCH is how high or low your voice sounds. Lower pitch sounds better. A higher pitch can indicate an emotional state.

VOLUME is the loudness or softness of your voice. This too can be influenced by emotions.

TONE is the sound quality of your voice. A nasal tone is sometimes associated with the whines of a complainer. The tone of your voice can indicate and be influenced by your emotions.

TEMPO / PACE are the speed of your speech. A very fast, incessant speech indicates a driven or nervous person. Speaking too slowly can be boring.

ARTICULATION is how clearly you sound out your words.

PRONUNCIATION gives an indication of education level and social status.

RESONANCE is the optimum pitch where your voice resonates and rings. It is a humming sound. When the sound vibrates, it should be in your lips and not in your nasal cavity. Your sound should be rich.

Humming can make it more and more resonant. If you breathe correctly, the voice will project further. You can learn to have better control over your breathing by practicing the following.

Ask yourself these questions:

Voice: Resonance is optimum pitch. It occurs when the pitch of your voice resonates and rings out. It is a hummm - hummm sound.

(1) Does your voice have life?

(2) Is it interesting?

(3) Is it honest?

(4) Is it expressive?

(5) Is it pleasant?

(6) Is it understandable and clear?

When the sound vibrates, it should be in your lips and not in your nasal cavity. Your sound should be rich.

Humming can make it more and more resonant. If you breathe properly, the voice will project further.

With resonance and projection, you can come to a sense of power and control over your breathing.

When you breathe through the diaphragm, you improve your speaking ability.

ADORNMENTS

The body in all its various shapes and sizes communicates powerful messages to others.

One of the most dramatic ways in which the body communicates is through the degree of attractiveness.

Both men and women have suffered untold pains for the privilege of being perceived as 'handsome' or 'beautiful.'

Reshaping the body to fit standards of beauty is recorded in both
historical and contemporary fashions.

Research in the area of attractiveness can be classified into three categories: 1) personality characteristics, 2) perception of the individual, and 3) effect of attractiveness on other's behaviors. The research is limited; however, yet ample evidence exists to suggest attractive persons are more socially skillful and more likable than less attractive persons.

Attractive persons continually rate higher on socially desirable evaluations such as credibility, happiness, intelligence, personality, persuasiveness, popularity, sexuality and success. When compared to unattractive individuals, attractive persons are perceived as having more fulfilling lives, happier marriages and more prestigious occupations.

Since attractive individuals are perceived to have more socially desirable characteristics, what effect, if any, do these perceptions have on behavior? Research has found that attractiveness has a definite effect on behavior in relation to courtship and marriage, interactive behavior and manipulation and persuasion.

Attractiveness correlates with greater persuasiveness in classrooms and courtrooms. Marriage and courtship decisions are based, in part, on individual attractiveness. Teachers, for example, interact less frequently and less positively with unattractive students.

Perceptions of the attractive individual and the effect of attractiveness on the behavior of others communicate important
messages.

Body image and appearance are also potent nonverbal communicators. Body-image research focuses on body awareness and body satisfaction with regard to how these factors affect development of body and self-concept. The degree of which individuals are aware of their bodies affects whether they experience depersonalization, body distortion or insecurity about the actual physical boundaries of the body. Awareness and acceptance of the reality of one's body usually produces a state referred to as 'body satisfaction.' The extent to which you are satisfied with your body may be related to events that occurred earlier in your life, such as being called 'four eyes' by peers resulting in a deflated self-perception in adult life.

Feelings of inadequacy and body dissatisfaction affect one's self-concept and consequently one's communication behavior. In addition, many therapeutic approaches are directed toward adjusting the structure of the body to release pent-up emotions. The basis for these therapeutic approaches is that the body is always communicating messages about the psychological and physiological self.

Body facial hair, height, shape, skin color, type and weight communicate messages of the body. The most abundant research in these areas is focused on perceptions of definite ideas about personality characteristics of a heavy person. Perceptions may not, and in many cases do not, correspond with actual attributes of an individual.

The communication process is dramatically affected by perceptions of the body. The human body with or without the adornment of clothing and artifacts continually communicates nonverbal messages. Although the body serves many purposes, research shows it functions as a major communicator about an individual's attitude, personality characteristic and self-concept.

CLOTHING: The most common form of object communication is clothing. The types of clothing that people wear are often used to assess, accurately or inaccurately, their personality traits. Social groups often use a common form of clothing to set themselves apart from other, presumably unaligned social groups. Object communication extends beyond clothing to other body adornments, such as wedding rings to indicate marital status, tattoos, piercings and brands.

Also included in object communication is anything used as status symbols. Most nonverbal messages of dress are unintentionally communicated and unintentionally received.

There are four possibilities:

ONE: the wearer intentionally sends a message that is intentionally received.

EXAMPLE: A prostitute dresses seductively to communicate her profession. The client can identify the prostitute.

TWO: the wearer unintentionally sends a message that is intentionally received.

EXAMPLE: You are interviewing for a job in a large company by a panel of two males and one female. You have deliberately selected your clothing for the meeting without paying any attention to your jewelry, which looks expensive. The interviewer assumes you are married because you are wearing a wedding band and in a middle to upper income family. You have unintentionally communicated a message that was intentionally received by this panel.

THREE: the wearer intentionally sends a message that is unintentionally received.

EXAMPLE: You are teaching at a college for the first time. You have, because of your young look, been mistaken for a student.
Therefore, you grow a mustache and wear clothing that is more expensive in order to communicate higher status. Consciously or unconsciously, other teachers and students react to the change.

FOUR: the wearer unintentionally sends a message that is unintentionally received.

EXAMPLE: You get dressed in jeans and a tee shirt. Other people unconsciously react to your dress. No intentional messages have been sent or received. Court cases make good examples of the intentional/unintentional relationship between sender and receiver. F. L. Bailey intentionally wanted to communicate that people like Patty Hearst were not capable of being a bank robber and radical.

The judge and jury unintentionally received this message. Why is this important? If you study the effects of dress in human communication, you will reduce the number of messages that are unintentionally send and received.

Effective Communication is conscious communication where both the sender and the receiver are consciously aware of the messages sent. Our choice of color, and hairstyle, is a means of nonverbal communication. Research on color and psychology has demonstrated that different colors can invoke different moods.

Appearance can also alter physiological reactions, judgment, and interpretations. As earlier described, messages can be sent intentionally, unintentionally, and are often unconscious. Of course, the need to know this information is to increase awareness of the communicative value of clothing in order to increase the chance of your giving and receiving messages intentionally.

A researcher named McGraw discovered that the self-esteem of the wearer is involved in clothing choice and cites this example: "When you know who you are, then you know how you look—all these little extras just fall into place."

You learn about your body. When people present themselves physically, you can tell how they feel about themselves. One possibility in analyzing the personality of the wearer is the selection of clothing in an attempt to project the ideal self. Additional research in this area reveals a more complex relationship between emotions, personalities and clothing.

An example is if you are in a down mood, you wear something you like or choose not to cheer yourself through clothing. Dress codes in schools and corporations are based on assumption the 'perceptions' of the public are important.

Research findings indicate perceptions are made and, in most cases, represent stereotypes about particular clothing and artifacts. For example, many police officers prefer to work in uniform rather than in plain clothes because they receive a more compliant response.

Using this same principle, try having checks printed as Doctor so and so and then go to a merchant and see if there is a reluctance to take your check! Dress has an effect on people. We perceive clothing to communicate messages and respond to the clothing as well. One of the more dramatic effects of clothing is the behavior of the wearer. If you wear an outfit you really like, it gives you a psychological lift and you perform better.

Clothing communicates a message and has an effect on the wearer. Clothing is a Language! What may follow custom in one part of the world may not be thought of as something appropriate somewhere else.

Appearances tell age, economic class and gender. If you put on a certain outfit, your behavior can change and others will see you differently in one outfit over another.

For example, if you are wearing a military outfit, this can change someone's feelings about you. This uniform/outfit communicates status. As much as 70% of the language we use is para-language.

PART TWO

GLOBAL COMMUNICATION

The single biggest problem in communication is the illusion that it has taken place.
-George Bernard Shaw

Here's the question: Which was right – the Indonesian concept of "rubber time" or the Canadian view of promptness?

Your answer, of course, depends on the cultural standards you grew up with –because different cultures relate to time very differently.

Body language is the management of time, space, appearance, posture, gesture, touch, facial expression, eye contact, and voice. The concept of timeliness is only one of the many nonverbal variants you encounter when doing business internationally.

Other variants include greeting behaviors (kiss, bow, or shake hands), seating arrangements, the way business cards are distributed and treated - and the amount of eye contact, visible emotion, and hand gesturing that is deemed appropriate.

Many emblematic hand gestures have cultural overtones. For example, what we in the U.S. think of as a positive gesture, the "OK" sign with thumb and forefinger together creating a circle, has very different meanings in other countries.

In France it means "worthless" or "zero," in Japan it stands for money, and in other parts of the world it represents a lewd or obscene comment. One of the most readily observed cultural differences is the degree of physical intimacy allowed or expected in a business meeting.

From *The Silent Language of Leaders: How Body Language Can Help – or Hurt – How You Lead*, here is how a dozen business people around the world answered the question: "How close do you stand in a conversation with a business colleague – and how often do you touch?

The United Kingdom - Brits stand at least 2 feet apart – and hardly ever touch business colleagues. Sometimes they might tap the table with a pen close to the person they are connecting with, but bodily contact is avoided.

Brazil - Distance isn't an issue for them. They can sit close or even stand very close to their business colleagues. Hugging and touching is quiet common in Brazil – especially in comparison with other cultures.

China - The Chinese tend to stand close in a conversation, less than 2 feet, but more than 1 foot. Sometimes, they touch the other person's arm or back or grasp a shoulder to show that they have established a trusting relationship. They may also bump into you while walking or talking. It's not considered rude in Chinese culture to bump into other people

Trinidad and Tobago - Certainly, men will not touch much, if at all; a pat on the shoulder at the end of a good meeting may be it. They stand about 2 feet apart.

Australia - Although known for their relaxed and easy-going countenance, Australians are surprisingly uptight about distance. If you stand closer than two feet it is considered intense and possibly an indication you are to be told something very confidential. Unless there was a pre-existing close relationship, an Australian would take a step backwards or sideways to create space. We are more comfortable with 3 – 4 feet apart. Australians would flinch or stiffen at a touch from a business colleague. Most male executives would be concerned about legal implications of touching a female in the workplace. However, a light touch on the arm or shoulder communicates that "I am like you, I am one of you," or "I appreciate what you have done."

Germany - Germans are more comfortable when keeping a good arm's distance away. And you won't see much touching, but it is more common in Southern Germany.

United Arab Emirates – People stand close as the concept of personal space does not exist and all transactions are dominated by relationships. In fact, if people stand too far apart it is seen as a negative and you can be asked why you are standing at a distance. However, not much touching happens in deference to the laws of the land where members of the opposite sex not related to each other by marriage are not supposed to touch each other in public.

Japan - They prefer to be 3 to 4 feet apart. 2 feet makes us feel uncomfortable. (A close physical proximity is unexpected except for the rush hour trains, literally packed with passengers, where we simply give up and accept the situation.) In Japan people hardly ever touch their business colleagues, but sometimes a male manager might pat his male colleague's shoulder for encouragement.

India - It is good to keep a decent distance (about 2 feet) during conversations and a demeanor that is respectful and a body language that is open (No folded arms close to the chest!). Moreover, when it comes to ladies, sufficient care needs to be taken on how close one wants to stand and talk.

In a business scenario, generally the only touch is a handshake on meeting and parting. Indians are warm people, and an innocent pat to congratulate or to ask someone to stop is not seen as offensive. A touch on the arm and shoulder is a normal trend, and a high-five among peers during a meeting is also a way of showing solidarity.

Tanzania - They stand at least a foot apart. We normally would touch/tap on the wrist or shoulder but very lightly.

Philippines - Two feet should be a good estimate for the Philippines, regardless of gender. For women, more senior executives would tend to be more formal and conscious of propriety. Touching is usually not appropriate among business colleagues in a meeting context.

Mexico - Mexicans stand close and constantly touch. If you don't know someone well, you'd touch mainly the arm, shoulder, and back. With someone you know better, sometimes you'd lightly touch the leg.

Developing cross-cultural savvy can be difficult and time-consuming. But not doing so can cost you everything. In Hong Kong, I watched a newly-arrived American executive meet with his Chinese team members, and I saw the new man destroy in five seconds the delicate and productive relationship that the incumbent had taken over a year to build. Undoubtedly the exec thought he was coming across as a hard-charging, highly successful leader. And that might have been the case back in the States. But in this culture, his actions were seen as rude, insensitive, and overbearing.

Like anyone else dealing with an international clientele, I have made my share of cultural faux pas.

One particularly memorable one was when I opened a global meeting with an "Ice breaker" exercise – a tactic that we in the U.S. are particularly fond of. (After all, "time is money," so we need to find quick ways to get this "relationship-building stuff" in full swing.) The audience gave a collective sigh, and then one European participant said, "Not another American ice breaker. Why don't they just wait until we thaw?"

International people have been extremely generous in overlooking cultural mishaps. They may say something like, "It will be fine, Carol. We know your heart is in the right place." So Aretha Franklin was right; it all starts with R-E-S-P-E-C-T.

If you show a genuine respect for other cultures' norms and values – even if you make an occasional blunder – it will be fine.

COMMUNICATION THROUGH LEADERS

The type of communication that is chosen is contrived for many professions, in order for the subconscious to get their message. In the advertising industry, plots are used to sell a product.

Have you seen a car commercial with a beautiful girl standing beside the car? Of course! This is what sells. We remember the girl!

Prosecuting and defense attorneys know how to '*play*' the jury with the nonverbal communication and use these signs during cross-examination of witnesses.

Silent movies and recently, the movie "The Artist" illustrate how, for example, eyebrows and smiles help in making movies.

Even the music in the background adds to the emotional impact of a story.

Silent movie star George Valentin bemoans the coming era of talking pictures and fades into oblivion and self-destruction, but finds sparks with Peppy Miller, a young dancer lighting up talkies like no one else.

Photograph(s) courtesy of Associated Press and Creative Commons Open Source.

The infamous photo of Michael Dukakis taken as part of his presidential campaign. *Photograph from AP Source*

Ronald Reagan came off as a wise grandfather as compared to Jimmy Carter, who seemed like a home boy. Reagan was also an actor and knew exactly how to work his audience, with posturing and intentional movements.

After the Valdez oil spill, Exxon officials tried to downplay the extent of the damage.

On May 19th, when Alaska retrieved corpses of tens of thousands of sea birds, hundreds of others and dozens of bald eagles, an Exxon had counted just 300 birds and 70 other forms of wildlife in order to minimize poor public relations for the problem.

In the 9/11 chaos, **Rudy Giuliani** forged a lasting image.

HBO, via Reuters

Mayor Rudolph W. Giuliani shown at the scene of the World Trade Center collapse on Sept. 11, 2001, from a Home Box Office documentary.

Nixon/Kennedy Debates

It was April 25, 2010 when The Wall Street Journal reported that on September 26, 1960, 70 million U.S. viewers tuned in to watch Senator John Kennedy of Massachusetts and Vice President Richard Nixon in the first-ever televised presidential debate.

The Great Debates marked television's grand entrance into presidential politics. They afforded the first real opportunity for voters to *see* their candidates in competition and the visual contrast was dramatic.

In August, Nixon had seriously injured his knee and spent two weeks in the hospital. By the time of the first debate he was still twenty pounds underweight, his stance still poor. He arrived at the debate in an ill-fitting shirt, looking very uncomfortable and he was sweating. He had refused make-up to improve his color and lighten his perpetual "5:00 o'clock shadow."

Kennedy, by contrast, had spent early September campaigning in California. He was tan and confident and well-rested.

In substance, the candidates were much more evenly matched. Indeed, those who heard the first debate on the radio pronounced Nixon the winner. But the 70 million who watched television saw a candidate still sickly and obviously discomforted by Kennedy's smooth delivery and charisma.

The television viewers focused on *what they saw, not what they heard.*

Studies of the audience indicated that, among television viewers, Kennedy was perceived the winner of the first debate by a very large margin. The fact is that we are judged by others over 93% of what we see (the nonverbal message.)

As the story goes, those who listened to the debate on the radio thought Nixon had won. Those who watched the debate on TV thought Kennedy was the clear winner. Many say Kennedy won the election that night. But television images were decisive neither in the debate (the first of four during the fall campaign), nor in the 1960 election.

David L. Vancil and Sue D. Pendell, in an article in the *Central States Speech Journal* in 1987, thoroughly dismantled the notion that disagreement among TV viewers and radio listeners characterized the debate 50 years ago

"The relationship of substance and appearance is complex, and the effects of electronic media on political communication surely deserve attention. However, there is little merit in speculation based upon unsupported anecdotes of the first Kennedy-Nixon debate."

Vancil and Pendell's research also challenged the notion that Nixon's haggard look much contributed to views about the debate.

"Appearance problems, such as Nixon's perspiring brow, could have had a negative impact on viewer perceptions," they wrote, *"but it is also possible for viewers to be sympathetic to such problems, or to interpret them as evidence of attractive or desirable qualities."* They added: *"Even if viewers disliked Nixon's physical appearance, the relative importance of this factor is a matter of conjecture."*

The fact is that communication, actually, changed a major outcome in the history of politics.

Bill Gates

Photograph courtesy of Associated Press and Creative Commons Open Source

Microsoft's co-founder Bill Gates, who is considered a brilliant technologist and a leading philanthropist, has not been known for his public speaking skills.

His Microsoft presentations were largely filled with mind-numbing statistics, highly technical jargon, and busy PowerPoint slides. That soon changed.

In early February, BusinessWeek.com's Innovation Channel editor, Helen Walters, blogged from TED, a prestigious annual conference where luminaries from all walks of life discuss ideas in the area of technology, entertainment, and design.

Walters noted that during his presentation, Gates released mosquitoes into the audience. But Gates' presentation on world health and educational problems was arresting for other reasons as well. It was passionate, concise (20 minutes), interesting, humorous, and engaging—everything that is desired in a speaker.

Gates' presentation style has evolved as he reaches for a broader audience. He said that only by getting people to care would he be able to draw in the governments, scientists, communicators, and experts necessary to strive for solutions to the very challenging problems he is addressing.

Gates realizes selling ideas requires more than facts and figures. A presentation must be engaging and memorable in order to get people to take action.

Steve Jobs

Steve Jobs will always be remembered for his work. For thirty years Jobs had studied and refined the art of effective communication. A Jobs' presentation was like a carefully crafted, well-rehearsed performance that tells a story and shares a vision. Gallo's book overflows with practical guidelines from Steve Jobs grouped into three parts or acts.

Act One: *Create the Story.* This is about preparation - the step that "separates mediocre communicators from extraordinary ones." In this stage, communicators determine why anyone would care about the talk. They select "one big idea" to leave with the audience, determine three or four key ideas to present, and decide on metaphors and illustrations that can be used. Every speech should pose a question or tap into a problem that needs to be solved. Then offer a solution, describe a course of action and call for action. Can this apply to church talks or to professional lectures?

Act Two: Deliver the Experience. This also involves planning. Slides should be simple without clutter, with arresting images and never with bullet points. Plan to do something different at least every ten minutes because that's when most minds drift away unless they are pulled back by something new. Consider ways to use demonstrations and props.

Act Three: Refine and Rehearse. Take the time to rehearse. When you speak, wear appropriate clothing. Remember that your stage presence can reinforce or undermine your message. And speak to the audience, never to slides on the screen.

Some of this is not new but it's worth pondering. Whenever I hear a speaker I watch the presentation even as I listen. As a result I learn to be better. Steve Jobs was a master presenter and an impressive model, worth watching.

SUMMARIZATION

Language and Communication can be quite complex.

Developing effective communication is crucial so that we can actually "be heard," when we have an important message to convey. No one will guess what you want or what you think if you don't tell them and nothing is going to change if you do not initiate a change.

Many people are unsure about the communication process because they may not be sure if they are sending the right message.

Once you have said something you can't take it back, so you should always be careful in planning what your message is and how you intend the receiver to "hear it."

Choose words that will express exactly what you want to convey so your job is to express yourself clearly in order for you to avoid misunderstandings. We must send our verbal, para-language and our nonverbal messages consistently. If we do not, we confuse the listener; often times and this inconsistency can indicate a lack of trust in some people and will undermine the opportunity to build a solid relationship. If there is conflicting communication, what is going to be believed is the nonverbal message.

If you see someone, for example, who has a clenched fist and they tell you they are not angry, you know they are not being   forthright.

Our ability to send accurate, conscious messages is just as important as our ability to receive the messages others send us. Through conscious attention to verbal messages, and the nonverbal aspects of our words, we are better able to communicate and get our thoughts and feelings heard.

About the Author

Dr. Joyce Knudsen received her Bachelors of Arts in Communication and a Masters of Arts in Business Administration, a comprehensive management training program recognized worldwide. Joyce has earned a Ph.D. in Human Services, with an emphasis on self-image and psychology.

Joyce takes pride in what she does. Her keen sense of business, strong educational background and support of her husband led her to the development of The ImageMaker, Inc. ® in 1985. This company continues to specialize in helping people to understand the importance of a strong and positive self-image.

For two years Joyce produced and hosted a daily television program, geared toward professional image enhancement and self-esteem. She has been featured in local and national newspapers, and has appeared on several local radio and television talk shows. Joyce now has her own radio show, streamlined worldwide at www.imagemakerincmedia.com

Joyce is a pioneer in her field having developed the first and only Home Study Mentoring Program in the world awarding 8 CEU credits by AICI (The Association of Image Consultants, International). She has the coveted distinction of receiving the first CIM (Certified Image Master), the highest achievement in the Image Industry, through AICI. In addition, Joyce was recognized at a banquet by her peers with the 2001 IMMIE AWARD (Image Makers Merit of Industry Excellence) for her work in the Image Industry.

Some of her interviews include USA Today, Glamour Magazine, New York Times Magazine, Indianapolis Star, Detroit News and Free Press and The Tennessean newspaper, Women's World and The Chinese Morning Press.
Dr. Joyce specializes in radio celebrity interviews, is an author of over 10 books and working with Image & Coaching Students, worldwide.

Joyce owes her achievements to a fundamental understanding of, not only herself, but others as well. Indeed, Joyce has learned what it takes to be successful – both in private and professional life.

By working with individuals, organizations and companies in many different industries, Dr. Joyce Knudsen is sharing her powerful insights into human nature. She is helping people to bring out their best in everything that they do. Joyce knows that happiness must precede success – that inner strength that we all carry within ourselves. She also knows that success is within reach of anyone.

You can listen to Dr. Joyce's radio broadcasts at
http://www.youtube.com/user/TheImageMakerInc

REFERENCES

Althaus, S.L. (2010). For inclusion in the Encyclopedia of Media and Politics.

Todd Schaefer and Tom Birkland, editors. Washington DC: CQ Press.

Massachusetts: Christian Science Monitor.

Brydon, S.R., Hellweg, S.A. & Pfau, M. (1992). Televised Presidential Debates: Advocacy in Contemporary America. New York: Praeger, 1992.

Gallo, Carmine. (2007). Fire Them Up! (John Wiley & Sons).

Kraus, S. (1996). Winners of the First 1960 Televised Presidential
Debate between Kennedy and Nixon. Ohio: Wiley, Journal of Communication. Volume 46, Issue 4, pages 78–96.

McClanahan, R. (2000). Word Painting: A Guide to Writing More Descriptively. Ohio: Writer's Digest Books.

Presidential Debates. New York: Priority Press.

Whitehead, A.N. (1927). Symbolism: Its Meaning and Effect. Virginia. Barbour-Page Lectures.

Wikipedia Varied Definitions (PLEASE NOTE: author holds no claim of accuracy for Wiki entries other than their validity on Wikipedia itself.)

Patrick Cramsie, The Story of Graphic Design. British Library, 2010

Rebecca McClanahan, Word Painting: A Guide to Writing More Descriptively. Writer's Digest Books, 2000

Alfred North Whitehead, Symbolism: Its Meaning and Effect. Barbour-Page Lectures, 1927

Jamieson, Kathleen Hall, and David S. Birdsell. Presidential Debates: The Challenge of Creating An Informed Electorate. New York: Oxford University Press, 1988.

Kraus, Sidney. Televised Presidential Debates and Public Policy. Hillsdale, New Jersey: Erlbaum, 1988.

The Great Debates: Background--Perspective --Effects. Bloomington, Indiana: Indiana University Press, 1962.

Minow, Newton N., and Clifford M. Sloan. For Great Debates: A New Plan for Future Presidential Debates.New York: Priority Press, 1987.

Journal of Communication. 46 no. 4 (August 1996): 78-96.

Russell W. Baker, "Critics Fault Exxon's PR Campaign," Christian Science Monitor (September 23, 1993). P. C3.

2002 Elsevier Science B.V. Vancil and Pendell: Central States Speech Journal in 1987

Related Website References

http://anthro.palomar.edu/language/language_6.htm

http://directionservice.org

http:www.tsbvi.edu

willaim62english.blogspot

www.businessballs.com

ezinearticcles.com (Dr.Joyce)

www.businessweek.com

www.eduqna.com

amarit04.wordpress.com

en.wikipedia.org

face-and-emotion.com

grammer.about.com

www.ehow.com

www.hks.harvard.edu

http://www.filmsite.org/afi100quotes.html

Dr. Joyce's Sites

Website: www.drjoyceknudsen.com

Facebook:http://www.facebook.com/#!/DoctorJoyce

https://www.facebook.com/DrJoycesBooks

https://www.facebook.com/pages/Dr-Joyce-posts-about-

Appearance-Behavior-and-
Communication/565756090163770

Twitter: http://www.twitter.com/drjoyce_knudsen

Linkedin:http://www.linkedin.com/in/drjoyceknudsen

Training: http://www.drjoyceknudsen.com

Presentation   Materials:
http://drjoyceknudsen.com/marketing-materials/

Radio Show: http://imagemakerincmedia.com

Blog: http://drjoyceknudsen.com/my-blog/

Ezine Articles: http://bit.ly/ppRgna

YouTube::http://www.youtube.com/results?search_query=J
oyce+Knudsen&aq=f

Google+https://plus.google.com/u/0/+DrJoyceKnudsen/post
s

Also by Dr Joyce Knudsen and available on Amazon:

From Head to Soul for Men, Daily Guide to Personal Style and Inner Self Confidence

From Head to Soul for Women, Daily Guide to Personal Style and Inner Self Confidence

From Head to Soul International

Successful Failures: Wisdom to Inspire You

The Generational Puzzle

Symbols: The Art of Communication

Mending Broken Hearts

And more!